HANGING OUT
with WILD ANIMALS

POEMS BY
CHERYL BATAVIA

DEDICATED TO CHARLIE
& GREGORY HORTON

HANGING OUT
with
WILD ANIMALS

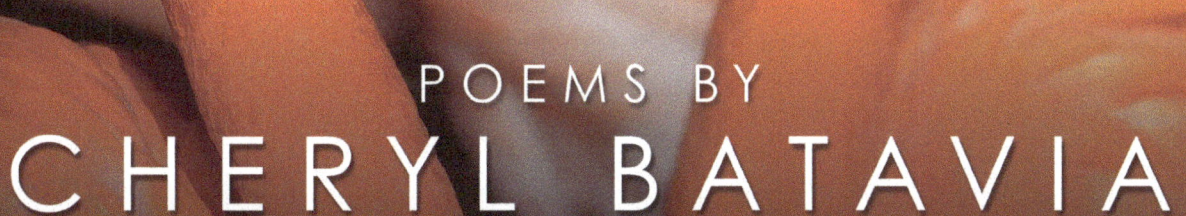

POEMS BY

CHERYL BATAVIA

INK START MEDIA
265 Eastchester Dr Ste 133 #102
High Point NC 27262

TABLE OF CONTENTS

SANDHILL CRANES, WALKING TWO-BY-TWO

In their own world.
Nothing else exists.
Ignore the people,
ignore the cars passing by.
Just you and me, Babe!
Foraging
beside the road.
Tonight we'll sleep
In the rookery.

MOCKINGBIRD

Mockingbird is doing impressions
of every neighborhood bird.
His impression of a whippoorwill
is the best I've ever heard.
I usually don't like imposters,
But mockingbird sings so sweet,
I'd gladly hear a mockingbird
on every single street!

DOLPHINS AT PLAY

Dolphins are like puppies,
playing in the sea.
They like to swim with people
and play around with me.
I wish I could speak dolphin.
When they come swimming by,
I'd ask them all to join us
at Manasota Key.

EVERYBODY CHEERS

Dolphins swim beside
our boat, they leap into the air.
Everybody cheers!

FRIENDLY DOLPHIN

Dolphins all have friendly smiles.
One even winked at me.
He swam along beside our boat…
Why didn't everybody see?

WHY DO FLAMINGOS STAND ON ONE LEG?

Why do flamingos stand on one leg?
I don't know. Look on the internet.
Where do flamingos lay their eggs?
I don't know. Ask the zookeeper.
Why are flamingos pink?
They're only pink when they eat shrimp.
(I read the sign.)
Why do people put plastic flamingos
in their yards?
Nobody knows… nobody knows.

PINK FLAMINGO

If you like pink flamingos, just think…
Flamingos eat shrimp to stay pink.
Without shrimp, their color fades.
Their feathers lose that hot pink shade,
so keep on feeding them shrimp!

BLACK RACER

Mosquitoes and gnats
buzzing around, being a bother!
Except for lizards living in our yard,
there would be many more.
Bugs are their favorite food!
A black racer lives here too,
and he has lizards on his menu.
Black racer is lightning fast,
but the hawk is faster
and likes to dine on black racers.

FLORIDA SCRUB JAY

Florida scrub jay habitat
is about to disappear.
Gopher tortoises and scrub jays
live in a preserve near here.
I've seen a lot of tortoises.
Maybe, while walking
in our yard,
a scrub jay might fly up to me…
I'll keep looking very hard!

EAT & BE EATEN

How many mosquitos
can a lizard eat in a day?
How many lizards
can a black racer eat in a day?
How often does a hawk
eat black racers for a snack?

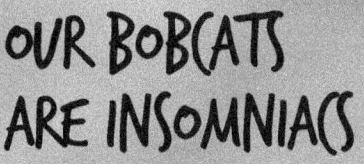

OUR BOBCATS ARE INSOMNIACS

Bobcats are nocturnal.
They just come out at night.
So why are they strolling
through our yard
when the sun is shining
bright?
I think they have insomnia
and cannot go to sleep,
or maybe they woke up hungry
and went looking for a treat.
If a bobcat is stalking our
hedgerow, looking for a bite,
I hope our rabbit is hiding
completely out of sight.

SHARK TEETH

Walking along the shore
of the Gulf of Mexico,
I collect shark teeth, artifacts
of a predator who lived
sixty million years ago…
before I lived… before
Native Americans arrived.
This fossil is what remains of the
shark's fierce struggle to survive.
Beyond my lifetime, shark teeth
will still wash up on the beach.
I leave behind… poems
and shark teeth given away.

RED TIDE

Exquisitely beautiful, gleaming silver,
washed up lifeless on the beach.
Little shark… so perfect…
How did you end up like this?
In only a day or two,
when the red tide came ashore
and made me cough and rub my eyes,
I knew, little shark,
what happened to you.

RACCOONS

Raccoons are cute and playful,
but they're also terrible pests!
They like to turn over the garbage
and make an awful mess.
It's fun to watch raccoons
play like monkeys in the zoo.
Enjoy the entertainment, but
don't let them come close to you.

ARMADILLO

An armadillo is a curious sight,
if you ever get to see one.
He tunnels in your yard all night,
eating bugs and grubs.
Next morning, you find tunnels
and a pile of poop
the armadillo carelessly forgot
and left for you to scoop.

I WON'T LAUGH AT PELICANS

Pelicans look funny diving
headfirst into the ocean
to catch a fish
in a silly-looking pouch.
But I won't laugh…
pelicans have been fishing that
way for thirty million years.
So I won't laugh
at goofy-looking pelicans…
If I had a long beak
and a big pouch,
I'd fish the same way they do.

PELICAN'S LUNCH

Flying high above,
pelican spies a fish and
dives into the sea.

FACE-TO-FACE

I stood face-to-face
with a hawk, neither of us
alarmed… just curious.

RED-TAILED HAWK

A red-tailed hawk sat in our lemon tree.
I gazed at him, he gazed at me.
His eyes were fearless, clear and bright.
I saw him up close, to my delight.
I was too large to be his prey;
He could not carry me away,
but his curved beak looked very strong,
and his talons were quite sharp and long!
Keeping a respectful space,
I marveled at his power and grace.
From his vantage point in our lemon tree,
I wonder what he thought of me.

CATERPILLAR IN A HURRY

While munching his vegetables,
is a caterpillar in a hurry
to be butterfly?
Is he in a rush to drink
nectar from flowers
and give grown-up life a try?
Maybe he just wants to open
his brand new wings… and fly!

BUTTERFLIES & FLOWERS

What's more beautiful,
butterflies or the flowers
that give them nectar?

SQUIRRELS' PEANUT FARM

My Florida yard is a peanut farm.
I know the squirrels don't mean any
harm.
The neighborhood's a sea of oaks,
but my neighbors are such generous
folks!
They have lots of peanuts they like to share,
even though acorns are everywhere.
The squirrels take it all in stride.
It's only a few more snacks to hide.
They planted peanuts outside my door.
I'd seen peanut plants before,
so I didn't pull them up in haste,
but let them grow till I had a taste
of peanuts that took me back in time…
Plant peanuts, squirrels; I don't mind!

ALLIGATORS LIKE TO BAKE

Alligators like to bake
along the shore of the lake.
If you think they're asleep
and sneak up for a peek,
It could be your last mistake!

FLORIDA SOFT SHELL TURTLE

People stopped their cars
to watch the slow progress
of the giant soft shell turtle
as she crossed the road,
heading for the little lake
behind my house.
A child could have sat
on her mossy green back,
but she looked fearsome, prehistoric.
Soft shell turtle, like the alligator,
seemed little changed from the time
when mastodons roamed
the Florida peninsula.
Good luck, soft shell turtle.
We're glad you're still here.

GOPHER TORTOISE

Endangered gopher tortoise
on his back, in the middle of the road,
in heavy traffic.
Was he trying to reach the safety
of the preserve,
or running away from home
when a car hit him?
Putting my emergency flashers on,
I stopped to help him.
I turned him right-side-up…
He seemed to be okay.
I left him close to where I found him,
going away from the preserve.
I hope he got where he was going…
and safely home.

GREAT BLUE HERON

Blue heron waded
out into the lake
and grabbed the biggest
fish he could take.
He coughed and gagged
and tried like heck
to get that fish
down his long, skinny neck…
spit out the fish and
exclaimed, "Goodness sake!"

Hanging Out Safely with
WILD ANIMALS

Some wild animals can be dangerous. Keep a safe distance. For example, an alligator may seem to be asleep, but can attack very suddenly. If a wild animal, especially a raccoon, approaches you without fear, it may have rabies. If a rabid animal bites you, you will have to get shots to prevent you from getting rabies. Your camera's telephoto lens is a safe way to get close to potentially dangerous animals.

It is not safe to touch many wild animals. The blue man-of-war jellyfish that wash up on the beach have a poisonous sting. Don't touch them, even if they appear to be dead. Most snakes can bite, even if they are not venomous. Turtles and lizards carry harmful bacteria. Always wash your hands after handling reptiles. Avoid stepping on fire ant mounds, or you may get very painful bites. Don't disturb eggs of sea turtles or birds.

It is sometimes not a good idea to feed wild animals. If you feed an alligator or a bear, they may lose their fear of humans and become dangerous. Then the animals must be moved or destroyed. Feeding some wild animals may cause them to depend on you and lose the ability to feed themselves. The food found in their own habitat is usually best for them, so avoid giving most wild animals people food. Plant a butterfly garden with milkweed and other plants butterflies like. This is a safe and beautiful way to feed wild animals.

Never release unwanted pets into the wild. Pet pythons that grew too large to be kept by their owners now live in the Florida Everglades, damaging the ecosystem and eating pets. Introduced species often have no natural enemies and can upset the balance of nature.